PASSIVE INCOME

THE KEY TO FINANCIAL FREEDOM 1

AMAZON FBA, DROP-SHIPPING AND AFFILIATE MARKETING

Table of Contents

SECTION ONE 2

    INTRODUCTION TO AFFILIATE MARKETING 2

    WHAT IS AFFILIATE MARKETING? 5

    UNDERSTANDING AFFILIATE MARKETING 11

    AFFILIATE TYPES 18

    HOW TO MAKE MONEY WITH AFFILIATE MARKETING 25

    CHOOSING YOUR AFFILIATE NETWORK 57

    WHAT TO DO BEFORE BECOMING AN AFFILIATE MARKETER ... 66

SECTION TWO 102

    INTRODUCTION TO DROP SHIPPING 102

    PART ONE 105

    PART TWO 108

    ADVANTAGES AND DISADVANTAGES OF DROPSHIPPING 125

SECTION THREE 132

    INTRODUCTION TO AMAZON FBA 132

    TIPS FOR PICKING A WINNING PRODUCT 137

    THE PROS & CONS OF FBA 151

AFFILIATE MARKETING

SECTION ONE

INTRODUCTION TO AFFILIATE MARKETING

Have you been searching for a realistic way to make money on the internet? Enough money to maintain a comfortable lifestyle, maybe even quit your job for good? Perhaps you're unemployed and desperate to find a way to keep your bills paid and caught up. We'll search no more. Affiliate marketing can be a very lucrative online business and the key to financial freedom.

The word "affiliate" means to be associated with a larger organization or business entity. The best part about being an affiliate is the fact you get to benefit from the hard work that has already been incorporated into making a product that is not only profitable but in high demand. It has been researched and tested. Before you begin your search for products to recommend as an affiliate marketer, there are three questions that you must ask yourself:

1. What are the benefits to others for purchasing this product?
2. Is it something you would buy?
3. Does the product you are promoting offer real value for the money to the consumer?

If you can feel good about your answers to these questions, you can proceed with the next steps to becoming an affiliate marketer.

There are thousands of affiliate programs on the internet, which can be a daunting task in choosing the best ones. My advice would be to search for products that are in high demand. You do this by conducting a keyword search on Google to find out how many people are looking for that product. Find this out by typing in "Google keyword tool" on the Google search bar.

A display box will allow you to type in keywords and phrases that people use to search for particular products and information. You can then identify businesses that offer affiliate programs that sell those type of products. Your only job now would be to connect the buyer with the seller through a blog or a website. Once a sale is made, you receive the commission which can be anywhere from 10% - 50% and in some cases even higher.

There is an abundance of free information about Affiliate Marketing on the internet. Although I suggest you do your research, don't delay getting started because you feel you're not knowledgeable enough. There will always be new trends to follow and more to learn. Just start and learn as you go. Find one affiliate marketing program and get started. Before you know it, you will be among those who are making a substantial income on the internet as an Affiliate Marketer.

WHAT IS AFFILIATE MARKETING?

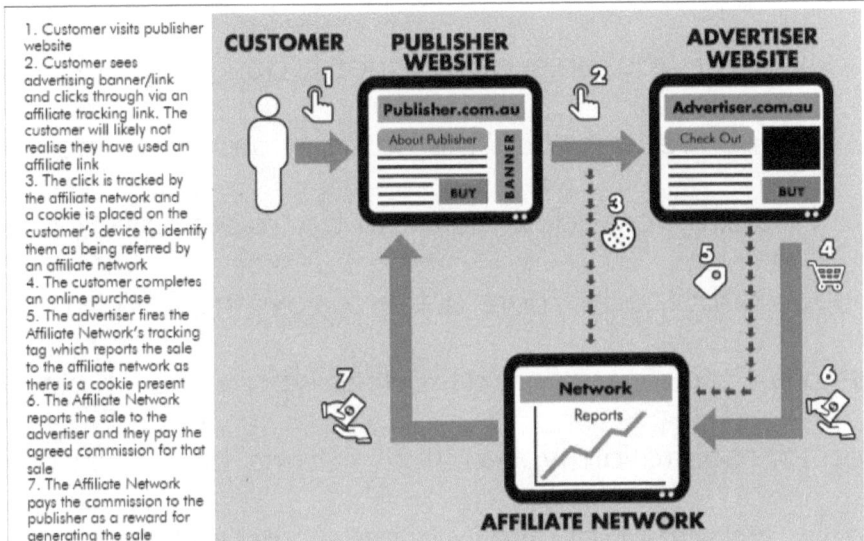

It's a good question, and one with an ever-evolving answer. So let's start at the beginning by trying to give it a simple definition:

Affiliate Marketing is the practice whereby a digital publisher or website promotes an online retailer and earns a commission based on the sales or leads that the advertising generates for that online retailer. We term this payment metric CPA – Cost Per Action.

Typically an '**Action**' is a sale of an online good or service, but it can also be a lead or registration, a call, a download or any other trackable action that is desired of the end customer. In recent years this has grown even to include offline sales — provided they can be tracked back by a coupon or barcode. There are two ways the CPA are set: Flat rate: For every action, a fixed fee is paid. This is typically used for registration type actions with no cost, such as a credit card sign-up or for a fixed price product like a mobile phone contract.

Revenue Share: The price of the item purchased is tracked, and a percentage of that price is then paid to the affiliate. This is generally favored by advertisers selling a range of tangible goods at varying rates, such as fashion retailers.

Affiliate Marketing is part of the performance marketing family, meaning the return on investment is guaranteed, and the advertiser is only paying for advertising that has succeeded. It's a versatile channel and is very effective at driving actions for merchants selling consumer products or services across a wide range of verticals, including apparel, travel, electronics, health and beauty, telecommunications, finance, and groceries. It should be considered as a vital part of an advertiser's marketing mix in an integrated campaign, specializing in turning brand awareness and interest into conversions towards the end-of-purchase funnel.

We use the terms **'Affiliate'** or **'Publisher'** to define the website that is promoting the brand or products. In later chapters, we'll look more in-depth at the business models that affiliates employ to drive actions for the advertiser. For now, let's dispel a common misconception: Affiliate Marketing isn't just banner advertising most campaigns will get less than 10% of their sales as a result of banner advertising. Consumers have learned to ignore these banners, so successful affiliates employ smarter, more engaging tactics to generate sales for the advertisers they work with, with most sales coming from 'text links' often hidden behind 'Buy Now' or 'Shop Here' type buttons.

A 'text Link' in the affiliate world is just a trackable URL that redirects to the relevant page of the advertiser's website. While the majority of affiliates still generate actions for their advertisers by promoting on their website or blog, there are now many other ways they create customers. This includes email marketing, mobile apps, paid search, remarketing widgets or campaigns, offline promotions, and social campaigns. The scope is almost unlimited.

Any publisher or partner paid to promote on a CPA metric could be considered an affiliate. How does it work technically? Most advertisers will employ an Affiliate Network to administer the tracking of their Affiliate Campaign. The network will provide a set of tracking links to the affiliates that sit behind the banners and text links on the affiliates' websites. When the customer clicks on that link, a cookie is dropped onto their computer, and the Affiliate Network registers that click. When that customer then completes a purchase and reaches the advertiser's confirmation page, the Affiliate Network's tracking tag is fired. That tag checks for the relevant cookie and if the customer has come from one of the Affiliate Network's publishers, the sale is recorded by the Affiliate Network in their platform. Via that platform, both the advertiser and affiliate should be able to see that the deal has tracked and a commission can be awarded.

The advertiser populates the tracking tag with all of the information relevant to the sale, typically the price and order ID are always included, then additional fields such the product stock-keeping unit (SKU) or promotion code can be added and tracked to assist with the analysis of the campaign's performance.

Again, there's a wide range of complications and options to improve on the basic tracking model. The more advanced networks can provide cookie-less tracking so that sales can still be attributed to affiliates when the user has blocked or deleted the affiliate cookie. This is becoming increasingly important as some browsers automatically block third-party cookies. More complex tracking can utilize unique promotional codes or block non-affiliate codes to record sales. Affiliate tracking pixels can be conditionally fired to de-duplicate against other traffic sources — through complex programming is needed around the rules for this, given that cookie, lengths are typically much longer than a single session.

UNDERSTANDING AFFILIATE MARKETING

The first question that most people raise when they approach this topic is relatively fundamental: What Is Affiliate Marketing?

Here's a basic definition that sums it up nicely:

Affiliate marketing is a way for you to earn money by selling a brand's products. As strictly a marketer, you have no inventory and work for commission. Generally, affiliate marketers receive payment when a consumer they referred buys a product or service or completes a specific task.

In other words, it's a way that businesses can outsource their marketing to you in a strictly performance-based way.

This offers companies a 100% return on their investment, which makes it unique among online marketing methods.

It also means that you have the opportunity to make a good deal of money by selling a product that isn't yours. The more you sell, the more you earn.

Moreover, since you don't have to worry about shipping, overhead costs, or customer service, your input is as small as you want it to be.

However, to make money as an affiliate marketer, you have to understand all parties involved and what they stand to get out of the relationship. Knowing each role and how they can potentially help you make money is an essential first step when starting as an affiliate. Your overall success requires building relationships that rely on three distinct parties:

Affiliate marketing at its very core is about relationships, a relationship between three parties:

Advertiser: The first party, typically referred to as the advertiser or merchant, is the party that's selling the actual product or service.

This is the party that you, the affiliate, will be working with. They usually have an established affiliate program, and leave it to you to carve out your space on the web and sell their product.

The product or service could be a physical product like phones or laptops, or even less tangible items like insurance policies. We'll cover many more possibilities and examine how to choose products wisely in a later chapter.

Affiliate: The second party is the **publisher**, more commonly referred to as the affiliate marketer.

This is you, the individual working with the merchant to sell in exchange for a commission. You'll have a contract in place, and you'll seek to push traffic in the form of links, ads, or in some cases unique phone numbers that you incorporate on your site.

Affiliate marketers fall under an extensive umbrella and could be just about anyone on the web. If you follow a blog or a popular social media profile, the chances are good that they are an affiliate of a brand.

The Advertiser/Affiliate relationship is a highly strategic one, as both parties need to make money for the link to continue. Since you're working so carefully, you need to be on the same page about your roles, responsibilities, and payment.

Consumer: Finally, you have the consumer or the party that will be (hopefully) buying your product. Thus, the relationship between the affiliate and the consumer should be one of trust.

The consumer finishes out the relationship triangle by interacting with your marketing efforts (like clicking a tracked URL or ad) and then moving further into the publisher's sales funnel. Once they've bought something or completed the action agreed upon by the affiliate and merchant, everyone receives their piece of the exchange.

All three groups center on the relationship created by the affiliate and will receive their product or payment through you. Of course, you'll also get paid when a purchase goes through.

Once you know how each party plays its role, you start to gain a better picture of how the entire affiliate marketing process works:

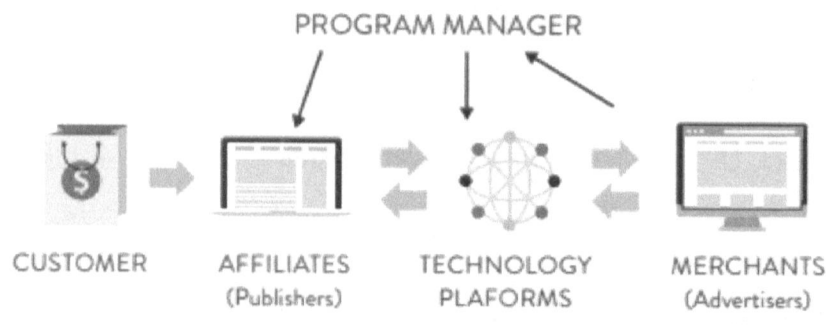

You, as an affiliate, publish ads or content that encourages a consumer to buy from a merchant. You'll have a set affiliate marketing method that will allow you to build an audience and promote to them.

Using various technologies and platforms, the merchant can track when you send a customer to them and will pay you if they buy a product or service. As a third-party to the brand, you have no say over what you sell or the price it sells for, but you also carry less risk.

When every aspect of affiliate marketing works together, every party benefits, consumers get their product, merchants generate revenue, and the affiliate makes a commission.

If you do this process well, you can make money in the long-term by keeping a consistent strategy and building stronger relationships with all three involved parties.

AFFILIATE TYPES

When we talk about Affiliate Marketing, it is essential to note that there are different types of affiliates. The method chosen by the affiliate to promote the advertisers' products is the key differentiation. Each affiliate type fulfills a different role in terms of value, volume, and reach. By understanding affiliates on an individual basis, advertisers will have the knowledge of who is best positioned to deliver in specific industries or to promote particular products.

Reward sites

With online shoppers becoming increasingly savvy, reward sites have seen a surge in popularity. This type of affiliate drives sales by rewarding its members through a share of the commission it earns from an advertiser. If provided with a competitive offer, reward sites can generate significant volume. They provide brands with an effective way to increase their exposure, especially if products are not firmly positioned on aggregator sites. If used strategically, reward websites can drive incremental growth (e.g., reward to increase average order value, higher commission for the purchase of new customers).

It is essential to have a sophisticated validation process in place to avoid paying commissions on canceled bookings or return purchases.

Content sites and blogs

These types of websites are often focused on a niche interest and feature unique content. A few examples are product review sites, blogs, and online forums. Often, Content Affiliates form part of an Affiliate Program's long-tail strategy and are rarely significant volume drivers. Regardless of their contribution to overall sales, they are valued partners. The reason for this is that unique content suggests editorial credibility and often has a positive impact on an advertiser's search engine optimization (SEO) efforts.

Content sites can also help reach a new audience. This audience might not necessarily be looking for your brand in particular but could come across it through a feature in a newsletter as the affiliate reaches an audience that is actively looking for the topic around your brand. A great way to engage and optimize activity with content sites is by providing fresh content or an exclusive offer.

Recently we have also seen an increase in integrated content pieces as well as affiliates who are using video to monetize a product.

Email

An Email Affiliate sends targeted emails to it is own (or third-party) database to drive conversions on behalf of a brand. To drive volume, a time-sensitive and robust offer is required, and creative should be refreshed regularly. It is essential always to consider the size and source of the data to ensure it is compliant with local and brand regulations and to avoid over-promotion or database exhaustion.

Comparison of websites

These sites offer consumers the opportunity to compare products of different advertisers (like credit cards or phone plans). Through a compelling offer, comparison websites can generate substantial sales volumes. They vary a lot on how they structure their rankings, which is not always based on the best product but often earnings per click (EPC).

Retargeting Affiliates

Affiliates retarget most commonly through tags that they place on the advertiser's site and try to re-engage with consumers who have not completed their purchase.

This could either be via an overlay when a consumer is about to leave a website, trying to persuade them to stay or via email if they have abandoned their shopping cart, making it easy for them to return and to complete their purchase. The advertiser has full control over traffic source and targeting options. It is recommended to trial different creative and messages and not to rely too heavily on handing out incentives.

PPC Affiliate

A PPC (pay-per-click) Affiliate is a search specialist who drives traffic to an advertiser's site by bidding on relevant keywords via a custom-built landing page. They generally work on a CPA basis but sometimes require hybrid commercial agreements. PPC Affiliates are not for every client but can be great strategic partners if:

- Competitors are cannibalizing advertisers' ads
- Limited budgets don't allow for an 'alwayson' approach, leading to lost exposure
- Aggregator ads are appearing on advertisers' search terms and directing brand traffic to competitor products

The key to a successful trial with a PPC Affiliate is to set up strict guidelines which help ensure affiliates are compliant.

Voucher and deal sites

These type of sites generate sales by offering their users a discount code that can be redeemed online against their purchase. They also often promote generic deals in a designated section. An exclusive code will usually increase exposure on the site, where a quick expiry date will create a sense of urgency for consumers and can be used as a strategic tool to drive rapid sales.

Social Affiliates

This type of affiliate works via highly targeted posts on social networks or sponsored tweets, which can help to drive awareness and assist in generating a need. It is essential to keep the creative relevant, with an active call to action.

HOW TO MAKE MONEY WITH AFFILIATE MARKETING

Now that you have a good idea of what it is, the next step is to find out how to make money with affiliate marketing. While we've already looked at some examples of businesses that have successfully done this, we haven't gone into much detail about how you get paid. This chapter will dive deep into the mechanics of how you sell, track, and get paid for the work you'll be doing.

This will help you understand more about what you're getting into, and provide some insight into how to make money with affiliate marketing for beginners. Knowing how payments work will even help you decide how quickly you step into the world of affiliate marketing.

How Affiliate Commission Works

As we've seen, affiliate marketers generally make money when they sell or help prompt the sale of a product, service, or other online good. This is also the general idea people think of when they hear the word 'commission.' Sales have to be involved.

However, that's only one element of how affiliate marketers can get paid. For the sake of simplicity, you can break down affiliate commission into three separate categories that work together to ensure you get paid:

- Payment plans
- Proven wins
- Payment systems

We'll talk about each, and show you how they work in your favor as an affiliate. The first element that you'll need to nail down when looking into how to make money with affiliate marketing is how often you get paid, or the payment plan. Generally speaking, there are at least three considerations when establishing a payment plan with a merchant.

Payment Plan Elements	How it works
Set Dates	Weekly, monthly, or quarterly payments. Often merchant-oriented to ensure adequate payments are made.
Minimum Payment	Once you earn a minimum amount, payment is triggered. If you don't hit this amount in a set time, payment delays until the next date when the minimum is met.
Sliding vs Normal commission	Determines if your payment is set, or can change with your performance.

When you establish each of these elements, you'll have a better idea of how you need to perform to gain a consistent income.

For example, if your minimum amount is $100 and you get paid the first of each month, you'll know how effective your efforts need to be to receive timely payments.

This also helps you plan your finances, and determine if the initial effort will be worth it. Once you know what your payment plan is, the next step is to determine which proven win you'll get paid for. While most people think about sales as the only affiliate marketing action that's available to you, your actual mission is really to provide a proven winner for the merchant. That means you can make money with affiliate marketing in a broader variety of ways than just selling.

A proven win is a much broader concept than merely closing a sale. That works in your favor, as it creates more opportunity for you to make money as an affiliate under the right circumstances. When a business tries to win a customer, they typically use a model called the sales funnel to help them create a systematic approach toward selling. Here's a typical example of what this can look like:

General Sales Funnel: 7 Steps

Generalized sales funnel that can be applied to any small business.

1. **Initial Contact** — Your first email, call, meeting or other contact with the lead.
2. **Qualification** — When you've determined a lead is serious and capable of making the purchase.
3. **Develop Solution** — Begin collecting facts about your client to develop a value proposition.
4. **Presentation** — When you've scheduled a full sales presentation, be it a demo or a written proposal.
5. **Evaluation** — When you address customer concerns about the product.
6. **Negotiation** — When you negotiate price and other details.
7. **Closing** — When the purchase is made or contract is signed.

Within this sales funnel, seven stages require a 'win' that the business has to achieve for a customer to make a purchase.

To make money with affiliate marketing, your job is to provide one of these wins to a business for an agreed upon price. Your affiliate commission is based on how well you perform this task. Since there is such a broad spectrum of set wins, you have plenty of options when determining your approach as a marketer.

For example, making that initial contact with a potential customer can sometimes be difficult for a business. If you can leverage your audience or a paid ad to help initiate a conversation between a company and a future buyer, then you can be paid for that.

In fact, there are a wide variety of wins that you can achieve in order to get paid. Here are three quick examples:

Proven Win	Description	Example
Form Submitted	You get paid when there are a certain amount of views of your ad, blog post, video, or social post.	You get paid per 5,000 views on a YouTube video. A video with 50,000 views = 10 payments.
Click, or X number of clicks.	You get paid whenever a visitor clicks on your ad, blog post, or a specific link in your blog post.	In your blog post, you include a link that nets $0.50 per click. If 200 users click, you earn $100.

Action, or X number of actions.	You get paid whenever a user takes a specific action, such as subscribing to a newsletter, making a phone call, or purchasing a product.	You run an ad promoting your merchant's product. Whenever someone purchases via your ad, you get 10% of the profit.
Demo Scheduled	For larger products and services, many brands prefer you set up a call with their sales team. Your goal is to schedule appointments, not necessarily sell.	You post a blog article about enterprise web hosting. Someone schedules through a link you provide, and you earn a commission.

Purchase Complete	In longer sales cycles, it may take more time for a purchase to be completed after you bring your customer to the merchant. This rewards generously for prospects you provide that actually buy.	A referral from your efforts negotiates with the merchant. After 3 months in their sales funnel, they close a deal and you are compensated a set percentage.

To make money with affiliate marketing, you will need to track and report each of these wins. As each is unique, you'll have to employ a variety of tracking tools to bring in revenue.

To give you a better idea of what that looks like, an easy way to track clicks or impressions is to create an online ad using Google Ads.

When you create, fund, and publish an ad, your dashboard gives you a day-by-day breakdown of impressions, clicks, and how much you've spent to win those clicks.

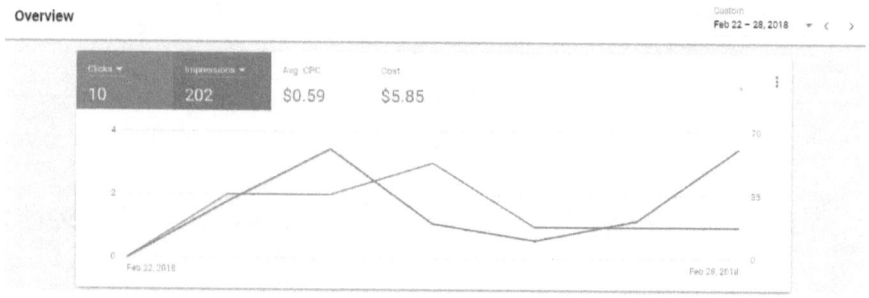

This is the information that you'll track and report to your merchant in order to receive compensation for your efforts.

Or if you're trying to track traffic to your site, an easy way to do so is to utilize the free tracking available on Google Analytics. Under the Behavior Overview, you can see a quick readout of how many unique page views you get per day, as well as plenty of other helpful information you'll be able to track and report.

You'll need to ensure that you're able to accurately track whatever metric allows you to make money with affiliate marketing effectively.

Moreover, in many situations, you won't have to track much of anything at all. For example, many affiliate marketers have issued 'specialized' links that act as a flag for the merchant to track. One marketer shared this example that he used as an Amazon affiliate:

http://amazon.com/exec/obidos/ASIN/0124211607/**wilsoninternetse**

The final, bolded element is his associate ID, which signals to the merchant which affiliate brought the traffic and needs to be paid for the click or subsequent purchase.

In general, you'll see more opportunities as an affiliate marketer under the 'Actions' category of proven wins. Since most trustworthy ad platforms don't charge for impressions, brands have moved away from paying affiliates to win those. The only exception would be brand-oriented blog posts or videos, but even those are uncommon.

However, once you've determined what 'win' you're going for, it's time to knuckle down and talk finalizing your affiliate commission. The next step of learning how to make money with affiliate marketing for beginners requires you to learn a bit more about how those commissions work.

In short, you get paid via an agreed-upon payment system. When it comes time to get paid, you'll need to negotiate with your merchant to determine what works best for both of you. Depending on your responsibilities and your merchant's flexibility, there are a variety of different payment systems that affiliate marketers use.

#1: Pay-Per-Sale

This payment program means that every time you complete a sale, you get paid. Depending on your arrangement, payment can be immediate, or on set days of the week, month, or quarter.

This system is as simple as a commission could be and is much like the traditional sales approach in that way. It's by far the most common type of affiliate payment system, and is usually the primary way affiliate marketing is represented.

Some companies even offer more complex sliding commissions, which means you get paid more for higher sales amounts. Under the right circumstances, it's beneficial to all parties and can provide excellent opportunities to make money with affiliate marketing.

#2: Pay-Per-Lead

Leads are potential customers that your merchant can follow up with, and can be of immense lifetime value to the right brand. Pay-per-lead systems are similar to pay-per-sale, except the 'proven win' is that you produce a qualified lead.

This is done through a process similar to pay-per-sale marketing, as it relies on audience analysis and delivering ads or content that are engaging. Usually, a qualified lead needs to hit a particular profile though, so sending any old point won't do. You'll need to ensure that your prospect hits all the right checkmarks before you send them on.

To win leads, you'll need to take a softer approach than if you were operating under a pay-per-sale payment system. Lead generation is more about gathering the information that your merchant partner can use to make a sale at a later time. That means using different tactics, such as:

- Email opt-ins or newsletters.
- Forms on your website or landing pages.
- Phone call scheduling.

Companies with bigger budgets usually run Pay-per-lead programs. For example, this list of pay-per-lead programs shows off multiple affiliate programs that offer more than $100 per lead. Most of the businesses require substantial investments of their customers though, so you know they can afford it.

This type of payment system is mostly used by companies that have a more offline-oriented sales approach, like car dealers or real estate agents. They can't make a sale online, but still, need leads.

In essence, this payment allows you to make money with affiliate marketing by bridging the gap between the customer and the merchant. If you want to do less hard-selling, this is an excellent system to choose.

#3: Pay-Per-Click

Pay-per-click is the third most common type of payment system, and it merely means that you get paid when your merchant's banner ad or link is clicked on your site. Since you get paid regardless of whether the customer makes a purchase, this has good potential. Unfortunately, as previously mentioned, it's hard to find pay-per-click much anymore due to some fraudulent behaviors in the past. Plus, online ads tend to provide a much better return on the merchant's investment.

#4: Customer Acquisition

This type of payment system is also known as a bounty program. The gist of it is that if you send a customer to a site and they make a purchase, you get paid.

While that sounds like pay-per-sale, it's different in one crucial way: scale. Bounty programs are typically used by larger businesses that bring in much more money per sale. They also tend to keep their accounts for a more extended period, which means the sale you bring in is worth more.

Moreover, it's also usually a much longer sales cycle. Here's a good breakdown of where this process falls in the overall sales cycle:

For example, a more extensive wholesaling website could pay an affiliate fee to a smaller client that refers to another business. You can almost think of it like a 'finder's fee.' Instead of making a hard sell, you only have to start the relationship between your merchant and the customer.

If you're looking for a way to make money with affiliate marketing that has high payouts, this option is an excellent place to start.

#5: Residual Earnings

The residual earnings payment system is much like the customer acquisition program, but the initial payment is usually smaller. Instead, whenever the referred customer makes another purchase in the future, a percentage of that goes to the affiliate.

This means your pay gets spread out over time and can be a useful method for affiliates promoting a subscription-based service. Amazon is particularly famous for taking this type of approach for their services like Amazon Music or Prime Video.

Moreover, if these subscriptions lead to more purchases, there's usually a little kickback to the affiliate marketer that goes with it. While residual earnings usually diminish over time, they can still add up to a significant amount and are an excellent option for affiliates to make consistent income.

#6: Multi-Tier Programs

In a multi-tiered program, the first tier is the same as any other payment system. You'll get paid according to your agreed-upon goal.

The big difference is that you can also recruit more affiliates. When you do so, you'll take a percentage of their profits, and therefore earn commission by doing virtually nothing. Theoretically, there's an infinite number of tiers that can get added.

Sort of like this:

While this might sound good, you have to keep in mind that you're primarily recruiting your competition. Combined with the fact that you're typically making a percentage of their earnings, you're getting a relatively small piece of the pie for each tier added.

Plus, there's no guarantee that the affiliates you recruit will make any money. These programs can fall short if you emphasize too much recruitment and not enough sales.

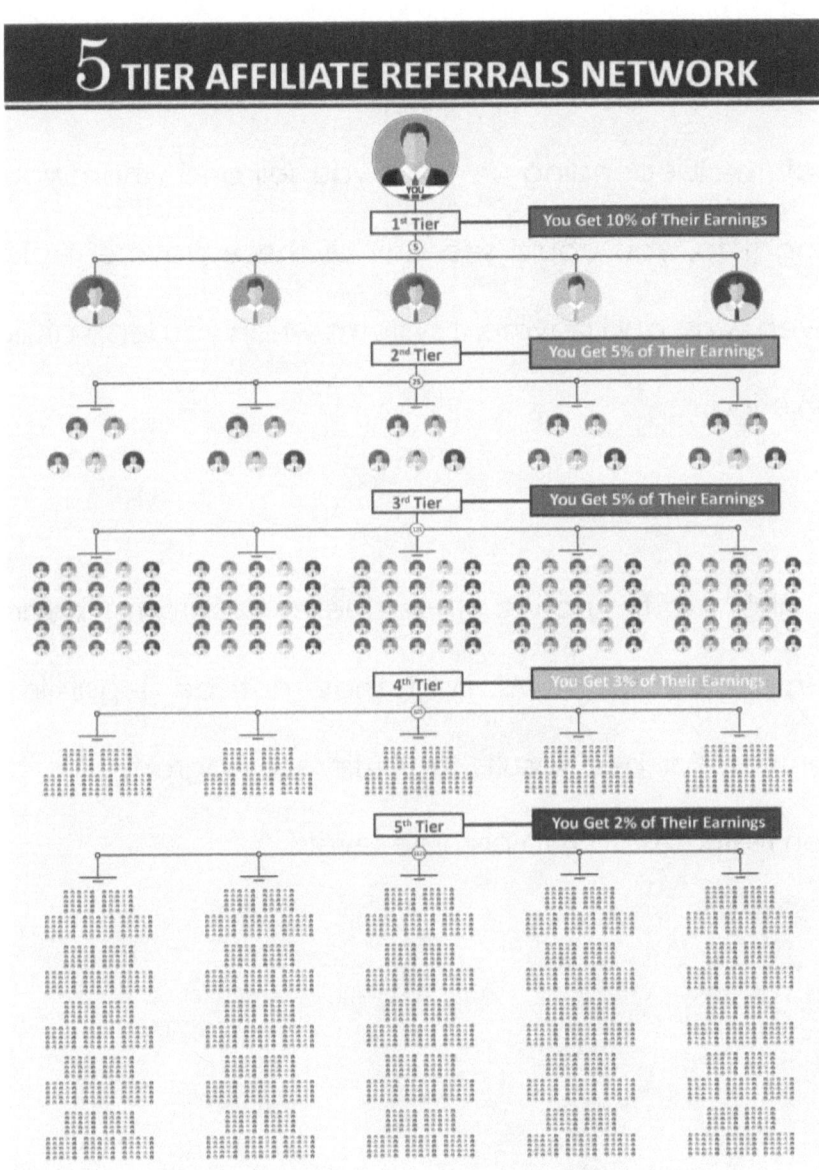

Reading the fine print of these types of agreements can help you keep from getting your hopes too high, and can give you a better idea of their ultimate worth.

Different affiliates and merchants will want different pay structures. Depending on what you sell and whom you're selling it to, you could see any of these payment plans, proven wins, and payment systems when you leap affiliate marketing.

It's also worth noting that these programs bear a resemblance to MLMs and may not be legal in all countries. For best results, multi-tiered programs are best when restricted to two or three levels.

Choosing the ones that fit your needs the best is the first step you need to take to make money with affiliate marketing.

Affiliate Marketing Average Income

Before you dive into affiliate marketing, you need to know if it will be profitable for you in the long run. That means learning how to track your return on investment or ROI.

One of the essential questions about how to make money with affiliate marketing for beginners revolves around how much the affiliate marketing average income is. This is the ultimate measure of worth, and not without reason.

However, if you're looking for an easy answer, there's unfortunately not one.

Becoming a profitable affiliate marketer is a tightrope walk, and is often a long-term endeavor. You need to be able to balance your costs against what you end up making, and that's not always easy.

For example, if you're running an ad campaign to sell a product, there are many considerations you'll need to take into account.

First of all, running an ad costs money. When you run an ad, you'll need to know your average cost-per-click, which means how much you pay when someone clicks on your ad. Here's an example of some average costs-per-click:

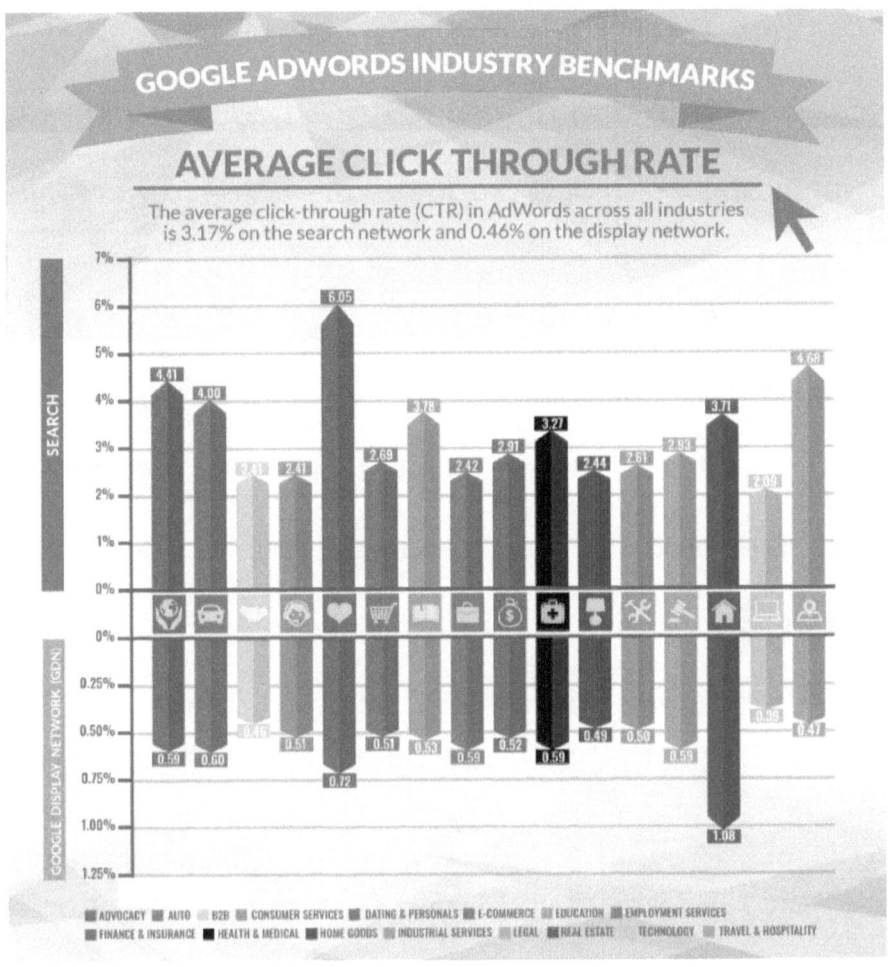

As you can see, cost-per-click varies from industry to industry. So when you set up your advertising budget, you'll need to take into account how many clicks you're able to get with the money you put in.

If four or five clicks can max your budget, it may not be worth your time and money to run an ad. You can take another approach or find another merchant to work with.

Then, you have to take into account how many clicks on average, it makes for one of those clicks to complete the entire sales process. If you get an average of one sale per every 50 clicks, then you know how much it costs to get a deal. That figure is called your cost per customer.

For example, if it costs you $0.50 per click, and you need 50 clicks to get one sale, then your cost per customer is $25.

If what you make in commission is less than $25, then your affiliate marketing average income is in the red. It's hard to make money with affiliate marketing when your costs are too high.

The key concept here is to find the right balance between cost per customer and the revenue you gain from winning a customer. You'll need to experiment to find the best balance between your expenses as a marketer and your income for proven wins.

For example, a recent study showed that most Facebook users only read the headlines of articles and ads before sharing with their network. That means focusing on headline experiments can help you.

You can also experiment with your ad copy, images, and the other elements of your ad to test and improve your click-through rates.

Then after you've run an ad for a few days, you can see the average cost per click in your Ads dashboard:

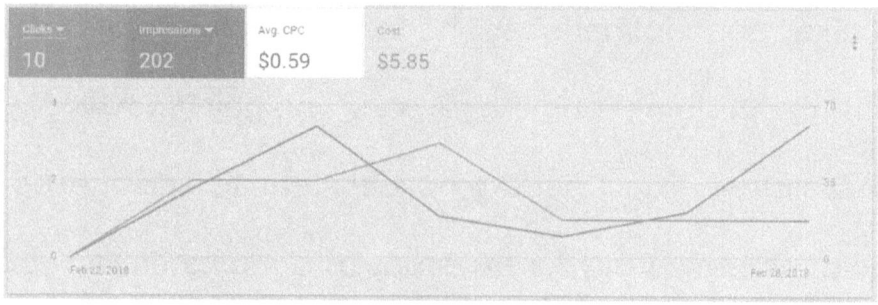

This will give you the figures you need to calculate whether or not running your ad is going to be profitable.

Also, this is just one example. If you go the blog-building route, you also have to keep in mind that building an audience takes time. While your costs are usually less, you still have to host your website and invest your time, which is no small investment.

From there, you also have the potential to run into the occasional drought.

One affiliate marketer saw an auspicious day that many only dreams of – $6,000 in one day.

The next day's haul? $0.

The truth is that there's no such thing as an affiliate marketing average income because it's going to be different for every affiliate marketer. Depending on your approach, budget, and goals, you'll see various measures of success and failure as you proceed.

However, when addressing how to make money with affiliate marketing for beginners, this is a valuable lesson. Don't go with what's trendy or what feels right. Go with something that's proven to give you a positive return on your investment in the long run.

Figure out the specifics of how you get paid to be an affiliate marketer, and then make sure your path forward is a good one.

Moreover, to help you make sure that path forward is a good one, in the next chapter, we'll look at some of the specific actions you should take before you become an affiliate markete

CHOOSING YOUR AFFILIATE NETWORK

Whether you are new to Affiliate Marketing or have lots of experience in the channel it always pays to weigh up the options between different Affiliate Networks and their strengths. Armed with the knowledge of some of the Network variables and what that means to your margins and ROI's makes an enormous difference to the potential of your program.

The benefits of Affiliate Marketing are many but none so great as the ability to pay commission to publishers based purely on performance. This alleviates the risk that if the traffic doesn't convert to sales you're not still being charged for the click or impression and the transparency of the ROI with the ability to track the origin of the sales.

Advertisers widely use the reason networks can be likened to any other form of business outsourcing where individuals operating alone can achieve more significant economies of scale. Additionally, systems offer extended services and technology - not least the tracking capability that is the core of the network but also billing management across hundreds if not thousands of publishers and anti-fraud and compliance monitoring.

BEFORE CHOOSING A NETWORK

Your aims, objectives, and strategy should be clear to you before approaching Networks and not allowing them to create a bespoke policy on your behalf without you being clear on what you want to achieve. As with any form of marketing the below needs to be considered and defined:

Aim

The aim is about identifying the reasons why you are entering the Affiliate Marketing space to begin with. It should highlight whether your ultimate goal is to increase market share, increase Sales, gain better ROI or only to create more brand awareness.

Objectives

Your objectives will go deeper into the aim you have specified. For example if your goal was more sales then you would define those numbers, such as, increasing sales by 15%, realized at about 500 extra sales per month achieving a Return On Ad Spend (ROAS) of 15:1

Strategy

Unless you are clear as to how you want your Affiliate Program to run this is where a network can advise of the most consistently effective strategy to implement. This can be in the form of a 90-day launch strategy where the system outlines clearly what needs to be done in each week to engage publishers and meet your objective. This will depend on whether you are managing the program yourself or have opted for the Network to manage your program, whereby they will likely have presented a Service Level Agreement (SLA) and agreed with you the strategy be implemented and roll out the 90-day plan on your behalf.

If part of your objective is cost-cutting measures, then it may be of interest to note that Affiliate Marketing can be integrated with other forms of online activity such as paid search (PPC), retargeting, and cart abandonment. Ordinarily, you might be paying for these services external from a network and instead could opt to run them through the Network not only for attribution but also to access them on a performance model the same as other publishers.

HOW DO NETWORKS CHARGE

The most substantial majority of advertisers that utilize Affiliate Marketing do so through an Affiliate Network that is remunerated primarily on a performance basis althoughmonthly fee's, setup fee's and sometimes performance minimums may be required. Advertisers pay a fee to the Network for the sales, sign-ups or leads that are accrued through the Network's affiliate partnerships.

The fee can be classed as an "override," 'network payout,' 'network bounty' or 'transaction fee' and can range from 1%-30% of any commission payment to publishers. This means that on a $100 sale you may be paying 10% commission to publishers so they would receive $10 of that sale and a network charging a 20% override will add $2 on top of the commission, making your total payout $12 for that transaction.

Types of Network remuneration include:

- Percentage of commission (example above)
- A portion of the sale value
- Flat rate per lead
- Flat rate per sale

Networks are negotiable on their fees based on their projections of returns and the information you have provided them.

WORKING WITH MULTIPLE NETWORKS

A recurring discussion by advertisers can be the question of whether they are using too many or not enough systems.

Sometimes the desire to add more Affiliate Networks to the mix stems from the belief that if you are using 'Network X' and achieving this result then adding another Network will double the results.

Unfortunately, this isn't always the case, especially within the same geographic region where the overlap of publishers can be high. Many publishers tend to be members of multiple networks to have access to the full spectrum of advertisers out there, so the overlap of publishers from one system to another may negate the desired result of adding another network and gaining a higher result than what is already being achieved. From a retailers perspective the benefits of belonging to more than one Network may be outweighed by the extra administration and duplication of effort

A multi-network strategy can be advisable when your online store or service is present in more than one country. Brands should bear in mind that the leader in their home territory might not be the right fit for their international strategy and may not translate to the same results they achieve at home. Equally, it might be the perfect fit and their knowledge of the brand and could turn into great achievements.

Brands should explore the market in the new country and speak to the partners available to them to make sure they're the right fit. Ultimately, their local knowledge will assist with program growth.

COMMIT TO THE CHANNEL

Affiliate Marketing is not a channel that is set and forget and to succeed it is essential to regard your publishers as a sales-force, which requires good communication, consistency and incentivization to perform effectively, regardless of the Network you choose.

Evaluate your knowledge and skills level as well as the resource you have available internally to manage your Affiliate Marketing activity will be imperative in the decision making process of which Network to use and also the level of service you will require them.

The combination of both a large and reliable network with a focus on technology (after all the Affiliate Industry is ever-evolving) and service will make your campaign attractive to publishers - translating into a program that is popular and profitable.

WHAT TO DO BEFORE BECOMING AN AFFILIATE MARKETER

Before we dive into some of the proven methods that affiliate marketers use to win leads and create customers for their merchant partners, I want to dive deeper into your responsibilities as you learn how to become an affiliate marketer.

If you stop to think about it, affiliate marketing is in some ways like starting a business. You have the distinct advantage of not holding inventory and typically don't need to hire employees, but you're still setting up an online operation.

And no matter what approach you take, whether writing blog posts or running ads, there are specific steps you'll need to take to help you find out how to become an affiliate marketer. That means you need to make strides to ensure you prepare yourself for what lies ahead.

In this chapter, we'll look at a step-by-step method you can use to learn how to become an affiliate marketer. This will provide a platform for your efforts, and can help give you a leg up when you're starting as an affiliate marketer. Whether you decide to go it alone, partner with others, or look for affiliate marketing jobs, these steps will prepare you for what's ahead.

How to Become an Affiliate Marketer

When learning how to become an affiliate marketer, it's essential to know where to start. It's all too easy to get the cart before the horse, and that metaphor covers a variety of scenarios.

Finding merchant partners, high commission affiliate programs, or affiliate marketing jobs that pay well and are consistent requires a great deal of up-front work before you're ever in touch with a merchant.

So to help you build your online audience and find the right niche, here's a five-step method you can use that can help give you a solid foundation as you start as an affiliate.

Choose a Niche

The first step of your training for how to become an affiliate marketer involves finding out which affiliate products to sell. To do that, you need to start with the bigger picture.

Every affiliate marketer has a niche in which they try to influence their audience. If you're too greedy and try to speak to too many niches, you could risk overextending and making your efforts ineffective.

So finding out who you're going to target is the essential first step. But just because it comes first doesn't make it easy.

Finding your niche is one of the most crucial parts of starting your affiliate marketing efforts. The wrong niche will make it harder to sell, and the right niche will make it easier.

So how do you find out which niche is the best one for you? To start with, you can do a short self-assessment. As affiliate marketers are meant to be reliable advocates for a product or brand, you want to make sure that you are in the right headspace.

Start by asking questions like:

- What topics am I passionate about?
- Do people search for my chosen niche?

- Will demand for my niche stay consistent?
- Is there a lot of competition for my niche?
- Are there affiliate programs that work within my chosen niche?

Even if you're creating and paying for online advertisements, your niche can make or break how successful your affiliate marketing efforts are.

These questions will help you find out if the product you're considering is something you want to promote regularly. No matter what type of affiliate marketing tactic you ultimately choose, these are the make or break questions.

It should also be said that passion shouldn't be the only reason why you become an affiliate marketer. A site like KitchenFaucetDivas probably didn't start as a project, but that doesn't make it any less profitable.

Someone has to write those reviews, right?

And the same goes for creating online ads. Someone has to create them and fund them, and not all of them are going to send you to Amazon or Home Depot. A simple Google search shows you that there are plenty of options for sponsored ads in this niche, too:

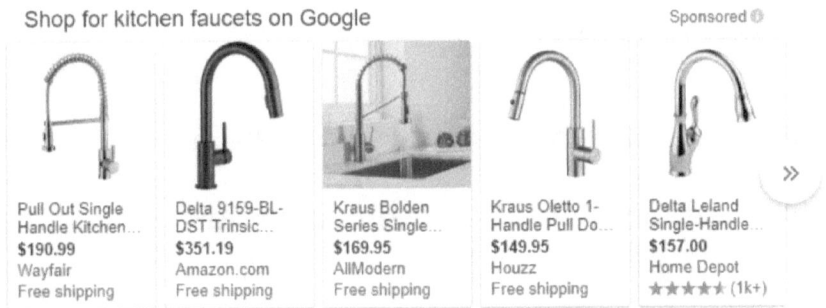

So keep in mind that finding the right affiliate products to sell isn't always about fun. It's about profit.

While passion can undoubtedly help you stand out, don't let it be the most significant determining factor in your search. Instead, base your decision off of the potential to be profitable in coming years.

If you don't genuinely think that a product will improve people's lives, don't sell it! This is critical to long-term success as an affiliate. It only takes one lousy recommendation to lose someone forever. But by taking the time to do your research, try every product you're thinking about promoting and think carefully about whether it's a good fit for your audience, you can build a successful business by being a trusted source of useful recommendations.

But you also need to know how to find the answers to some of the questions I've just presented to you. For example, how do you determine if demand will stay consistent? You don't have a crystal ball, and you're new to this process.

So while I can't help you determine if you're passionate about something, I can help you answer the rest of the questions on the list above to help you see how to become an affiliate marketer.

To start assessing demand for a product, the best place to go is usually a tool like Google Trends. This tells you how often Google users search for a particular topic on a 0-100 scale. It also gives you a regional breakdown, and some suggested topics as well. For example, let's see how many people search for the phrase 'kitchen faucet' on Google:

It's relatively consistent, between the '70s to '90s. That means those kitchen faucet reviews have an excellent potential to make money through affiliate marketing.

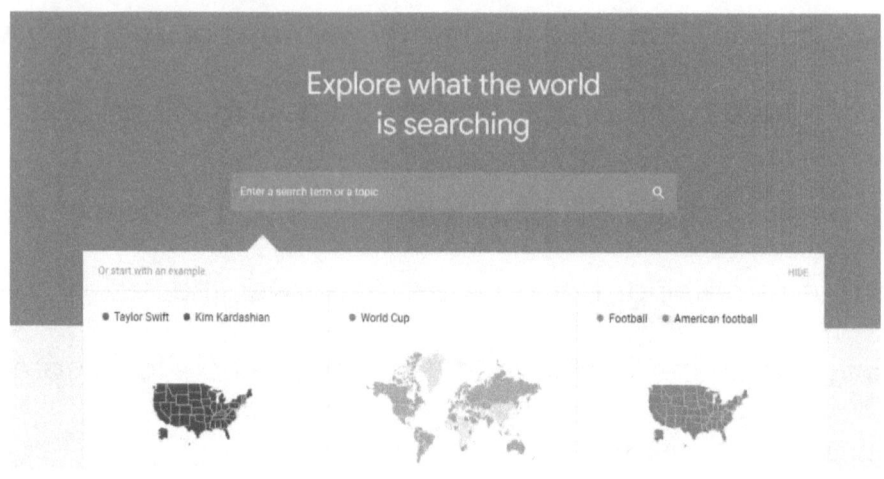

So whatever niche you're considering, start by plugging it in and seeing if there's consistent demand. This is one of the most consistent tests you can run when determining which affiliate products to sell. Many affiliate marketing items will have moderate degrees of consistency, with spikes around the holidays.

A good example is a quick search for 'watches.'

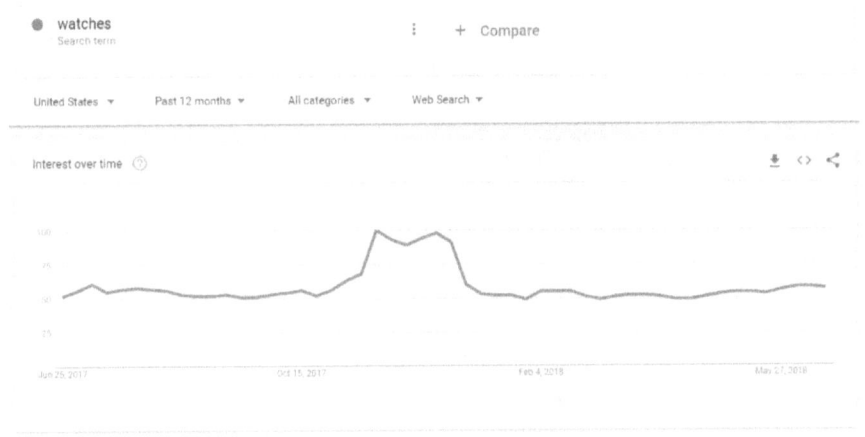

You may or may not see success with niches like this, so take this type of result with a grain of salt. You'll need to dig deeper to see if this niche will work for you.

But this does effectively answer the second question of consistency in your niche as well. Google Trends gives you two birds with one stone, so use it liberally as you study how to become an affiliate marketer.

The next step is to determine whether or not there's a lot of competition in your chosen niche, and there are a couple of ways to go about this.

A simple way is to use a keyword research tool like Ubersuggest to help you see how competitive particular Google searches are.

Let's keep running with this kitchen faucet example, to show you how it works. Start by plugging in your search term, and then click 'Look Up' to see the results.

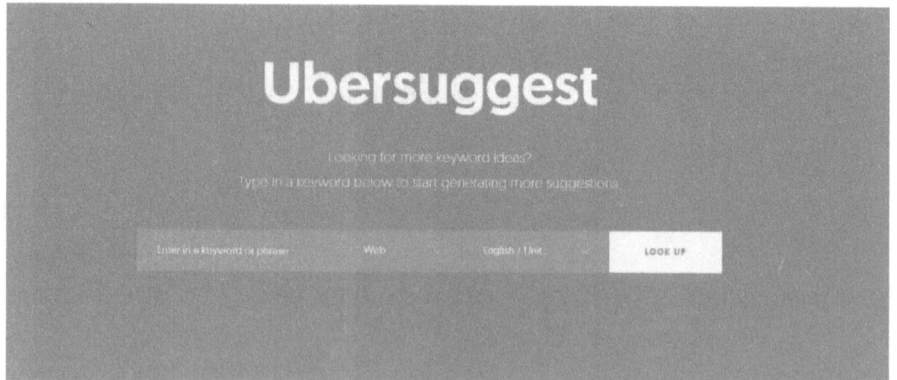

As you can see, on the right side of the results, you'll see an indicator that says 'Competition.' On Ubersuggest, this indicator ranges from 0-1, with 1 being the highest level of competition.

So with just a few clicks, you can find out what you're up against in your niche. You can also see a variety of suggested searches that are related to your niche, as well as how competitive they are.

The second way to research competition levels is to use a service like Clickbank. From there, you'll see an option to input a search term. Again using the kitchen faucet as an example, here's how you use this feature:

On ClickBank, Gravity is a measurement of how high demand is for a product that's on a 100 point scale. The lower the Gravity, the harder it will be to sell your product.

When you combine all of these approaches, you should be able to get an adequate view of how well your chosen niche will perform. Too much competition and not enough demand is a recipe for disaster, so be diligent in this process.

An excellent example of an affiliate marketer that's done their homework in their niche is the highly successful site the Points Guy. The site centers around travel-oriented reviews and guides, but also provides curated news updates for those already on the go. They also promote credit cards, which is where they make their money.

This site gets more than 2.5 million unique monthly visitors, and for every successful card signed up for, they receive anywhere from $50-$400. As both the travel industry and the credit card industry can be competitive, this is the kind of success that makes you pay attention.

The Points Guy | Get the Most from Your Card
[Ad] www.thepointsguy.com/ ▼
A Trusted Voice In Rewards Credit Cards. Find The One For You & Apply Today!

Best Premium Travel Cards
Find Your Ideal Premium Credit Card
We Compare Card Benefits For You.

Top Travel Rewards Cards
See Our Top Travel Rewards Cards,
Ranked By Signup Bonus & Perks

Beginner's Points Guide
New to Points & Airline Miles?
Check Out Our Beginner's Guide

Credit Card Reviews
In-Depth Reviews of Top-Rated Cards
Hotel, Airline & Travel Cards

And to round out their approach, they also run ads for their content to help bring in more traffic and make more money.

At the very least, this shows the importance of finding the right affiliate products to sell in your niche. Get this step right, and you'll be giving yourself the best chance to make some money as an affiliate marketer.

But the process doesn't end here. Your next step is to find an affiliate program that will take you one step closer to finding the merchant partners who will provide the products you promote and compensate you for your efforts.

Research Programs

After you've picked a niche, the second step is to find out which program out there can help you promote products in your niche. This is where you take a step deeper into your study of how to become an affiliate marketer.

Affiliate marketing programs are sites that act as the middleman between merchants and affiliates. Since it can be hard for merchants and affiliates to find each other, these sites act as a gateway for the relationship to begin.

Since program research is such an in-depth discussion, we've devoted an entire chapter to it later on in this guide.

But for now, I'll at least bring up some key questions that you'll need to have answered while you're figuring out how to become an affiliate marketer. This an essential checklist that you should consider before you proceed with a particular program.

What merchants are using the affiliate program you're looking at?

How much commission are you likely to make from your program?

Do you want to be associated with the program, and the brands selling through it?

What kind of support does the program provide you with?

Keep in mind that this is another step that can make or break your success as an affiliate marketer. Your program is the bridge that helps you find profitable partnerships, so don't skip out on it.

Build Your Platform

The first two steps in this section focus on assisting you research. From here on out, you'll get to start creating the platform that helps you succeed as you learn how to become an affiliate marketer.

In the first chapter, I shared the two most popular ways that affiliate marketers work:

- Websites like blogs or marketplaces.
- Paid ads.

While these are only a couple of options, they're the place that most affiliate marketers go. So in this section, we'll break down how to set up each.

First up, let's build a website.

While there's some discussion over whether or not affiliates need a website at all, there are so many benefits that it's almost pointless not to make one when you're trying to get the knack of how to become an affiliate marketer.

It doesn't matter if you're working with low or high commission affiliate programs, websites can help you be successful.

Plus, if you want to look for affiliate marketing jobs in the future, having your affiliate site is a perfect resume builder.

So when you search for ways to build a website, you're going to get a lot of competing opinions about which option is the best. Should you go with a free option like Wix or WordPress.com, or is it better to build your own by using a hosting service and going with WordPress.org?

The ultimate choice is up to you, but by far the better option for growth is a hosted WordPress.org site. You've got more flexibility, and you stand a better chance of being found via a search engine.

So to get things started, you'll want to sort out your hosting. There are plenty of great options for hosting, like HostGator, Bluehost, or GoDaddy, to help you get started quickly and affordably. While the ultimate hosting choice is up to you, you'll want to find one that offers reliable service and a good experience all around.

Many of these hosting companies offer:

- Reliable hosting
- A domain name
- WordPress.org integration
- A professional email address

And if you're feeling overwhelmed by the process of starting a website, some of these services even offer step-by-step tutorials on their site that help gets you started.

If you're starting a blog, your best bet is to find a template theme that helps you create a friendly user experience. There are thousands of items to choose from, so pick the one that suits you best.

The easiest way to set up a theme is to find it in your WordPress dashboard under the Appearance tab:

- This will give you the ability to install the theme of your choosing with just a few clicks.
- And if you want to make the website building process easy, it's also a good idea to utilize a drag and drop style theme like the ones offered by Themify. You may have to pay a little extra for them, but it makes everything much more comfortable.
- Once you host your site and pick a theme, all you have left to do is design it to your liking. You can use custom or stock photos, and make sure that it's clear what your site has to offer your audience.

From there, it's time to start creating the content you want to share with your audience.

Create and Publish Top-Notch Content

Creating content is one of the final steps of your pre-affiliate journey. In that way, it's also the gateway to the start of your affiliate marketing efforts. It doesn't matter if you're blogging or publishing ads when you've hit this phase you're in the home stretch of learning how to become an affiliate marketer.

The phrase 'content is king' gets thrown around a lot in marketing, and there's a good reason for that. In many ways, the Internet is just a collection of content. If you don't contribute, people have no right to come to you.

As we've already seen, that content can be as simple as an ad, or as complex and in-depth as this very ebook. How you ultimately deliver value is up to you.

But what types of content can you create that will help you stand out as a trustworthy and valuable affiliate marketer? Even if you've got the right niche and a flawless website, you need something to build your audience.

When considering what type of content to create, you've got a lot of options. One blog compiled 113 different types of content that can be created and shared. With all that variety, where do you start?

While to some degree, this boils down to the ideas that interest you the most, there are at least three right starting places familiar to affiliate marketers. These can ultimately lead to success, so we'll dive into each.

Product Reviews

One of the most common models marketers use when learning the ropes of how to become an affiliate marketer is to write reviews for different products and services in their niche. Ecommerce sites are always looking for product reviews that convert customers, so this can be a profitable place to start.

When done well, it can provide a seamless transition into affiliate marketing efforts, and can be a great way to generate income.

For example, TheBestVPN is a site that reviewed the most popular Virtual Private Networks, or VPNs, on the market. For audiences interested in cybersecurity and ensuring the protection of their information, this type of website is a goldmine of information.

With each review, there's an option for readers to go to the site and learn more about the VPN. As you might expect, this link is an affiliate link that attributes each referred buyer to TheBestVPN's website.

By solely focusing on product reviews, the site positions itself as a high-authority source for newcomers to the world of cybersecurity. Everyone involved gets something from the affiliate relationship, which completes the perfect model of affiliate marketing.

Blog Posts

In a similar vein to product reviews, blog posts are another way that you can start building trust and making inroads in your chosen niche. More importantly, blog posts can help you boost sales over time as you master how to become an affiliate marketer, which is your end goal.

By addressing common questions or problems in your target market, you'll be positioning yourself to make recommendations down the line.

The big key to writing blog posts is consistency. You need to post consistently, and you need to keep a single voice that provides high-quality ideas and tips to your reader.

An excellent affiliate brand that's done an excellent job of developing an innovative blogging approach is the site Top Ten Reviews.

While it sounds at first glance that this is just another review site, it's a lot deeper than that. It's a review comparison site that's all delivered in blog posts and slideshares, like this roundup on iOS apps:

- By creating and providing unique content, they've developed an engaged audience and dominate their niche. All of this is done as an affiliate too.
- So if you're struggling with a place to start and don't want to do product reviews, take the leap into blogging. Offer solutions and share your tips as much as possible.

Guides

The final type of content you can focus on creating is an informational product that you can use as a hook to get people interested in more of what you have to say. Just like the previous two types of content, helpful guides can ultimately lead to increased sales and more money in your pocket.

This can be an ebook, email series, webinar, or any other type of long, in-depth look at a particular topic. As long as it's accurate and helpful, you'll be one step closer to gaining trust in your niche.

In time, you can also use this technique to help your audience build interest in the affiliate product that you sell.

A good, simple example of this comes from the affiliate blog PC Part Picker. They offer a wide variety of guides that help newcomers and veterans build a computer that meets their needs.

This provides constant engagement with their audience with high-value content. And of course, with each purchase made from their recommendation, The Wire Cutter gets a piece as the affiliate marketer.

Create Your Ad Account

As we've seen all along, building a website is just one option when considering how to become an affiliate marketer. Ads are an excellent marketing method that can help you be successful, especially for high commission affiliate programs.

So what if you only want to use paid ads to push people to your merchant partner's site? In that case, you don't need a website.

Instead, you'll need to set up an account to create ads in, which means you'll need to use Google ads, Facebook ads, or even Bing ads depending on your audience.

So first off, let's show you how to get started on Google Ads. To get started, you'll need to head over to the Google Ads homepage and click the Get Started button.

You'll be sent to a screen that asks for your email address and the website you'll be posting ads to.

Next, you'll be asked to sign in if you're creating this with a Google account.

From there, you'll be walked through the process to target and complete your ad, including images and copy. First, you'll need to pick a goal for your ad.

Since you're most likely trying to get users to buy a product, you'll want to select the 'Take action on your website' option. Even if you're not the website's owner, you can direct and track traffic accordingly.

From there, you'll need to select the geographical location that you want to advertise. This can be as broad or as narrow as you want it to be.

Once you've pinned down the location, you'll want to define further what it is you're selling. Based on the content of the website, Google Ads will suggest products and services you can include that help narrow or expand your audience.

Once you've finished defining your product or service, the next step is to create the final ad. On the next screen, you'll be able to edit the copy of your commercial and finalize how it appears on a search engine results page.

Once you're done, all that's left is to finish publishing your ad and make adjustments as needed. At this point, you'll have successfully created both your platform and your content.

Another great option is to set up Facebook Ads to reach your audience as well. All you need to do that is a Facebook profile, which you may already have. If not, it's easy to set one up.

Once you've logged into your Facebook account, head over to the dropdown menu in the top right of your Newsfeed, you'll want to click the "Create Ads" option.

This will redirect you to Facebook's dedicated Ad Manager. There's plenty to explore and experiment with, but your first step is to set up your ad. Much like Google Ads, you'll be walked through that process starting from the home screen. Just find this section to get started:

You'll select your objective, create your ad, and fine-tune your schedule and budget based on your experimentation. Much like Google Ads, you'll need to take some time to familiarize yourself with the platform and what your audience is looking for.

But not all ads are the same. Just like blog content, there are different ways you can approach creating an ad. To give you an example, let's look at one of the options Google has to offer.

Google Shopping Ads

I've mentioned all along that blogging is only one option when learning how to become an affiliate marketer. You have ads, videos, images, and a multitude of other options that will help you build an audience and sell products effectively.

Since ads are by far one of the more popular ways affiliate marketing content gets created and shared, it's worth taking a more extended look at your content options that maximize their effect. And since your task as an affiliate marketer is to sell products, what better way to do it than with Google Shopping Ads?

Google Shopping Ads are the options you see at the top of the search engine results page when you're looking for a particular product. Here's an example of what that could look like when searching for some men's shirts:

This type of ad content can help you stand out and tap into your audience's desire for visual content. Some companies report a 1,800% return on investment for this type of ad. Your mileage may vary, but it's a clear winner for your ad content needs. While the type of ad you create and promote is mainly dependent on your niche, the key takeaway is that you need to create something compelling. It's the final crucial step in mastering how to become an affiliate marketer.

Finding merchants to partner with, high commission affiliate programs, or profitable affiliate marketing jobs hinges on the steps outline above. No matter what your goal is, the steps in this chapter can help make your journey as an affiliate marketer much more comfortable in the long run.

DROP SHIPPING

SECTION TWO

INTRODUCTION TO DROP SHIPPING

Dropshipping is the hassle-free way to make money from eBay, and it carries several distinct advantages for people who are just starting up. With drop shipping, you only pay for the goods you have sold through your store, freeing up working capital to keep your business ticking over. A third party stocks and ships your products on your behalf to customers through services like AliExpress. So what are you waiting for? Here's how you can dropship your way to financial freedom.

Choosing A Product Niche

In the first instance, you may need to test a few different markets before you find your financial 'sweet spot.' That is the products that bring in the highest sales figures within a niche that is popular, but not wholly over-saturated.

Sourcing Products

In searching for the products you wish to sell online, consider the product pricing and profit margins. This will be key to determining the speed with which you can grow your dropshipping business. Remember, in the journey to making your first million, and it's a lot easier to sell 10,000 units of a $100 product than it is to sell 100,000 units of a $10 product.

Consider Selling Through Alternative Channels

Look at listing your goods on alternative marketplaces like Etsy to utilize the traffic on these massive sites for your brand. Standing out from the competition hinges on your ability to maximize the appeal of your product listing.

Change your titles and descriptions to optimize for 'best match' using Title Builder.

Marketing Your Ecommerce Store

Next, you will want to set up paid advertising campaigns on Facebook to help you bring in customers. Facebook allows you to target your ad campaigns to highly specialized audiences. Set up a page for your brand and head to the 'campaigns' tab to set up your advertising. Look back at your previous research to come up with content ideas. Vary the headlines, images, and messages, and test them using Facebook Insights to discover which ads draw the most traffic to your store.

Maintaining Smooth Operations In Your Store

eBay store creators can also access an extensive catalog of useful plugins designed to make your life as an online shopkeeper easier.

Dropshipping your way to financial freedom through services like eBay and Amazon hinges on your ability to come across as an honest and reputable seller who is there to meet your customers' needs. With proper research, access to accurate sales figures and a right eye for trends, you can build a profitable eBay business in the space of a few weeks.

PART ONE

The Basics

According to Entrepreneur Magazine, there are seven basic requirements that you must meet to begin working as a dropshipping professional:

1. Choose a product to sell
2. Locate a supplier who will dropship for you

3. Set up an account with the dropshipper
4. Advertise the product for sale (they suggest eBay, but you can use Amazon.com, your website or a web store)
5. Use an online processor to accept instant payments
6. Order through the dropshipper (your supplier)
7. Follow up after every sale.

Think of these things like a good foundation, but also consider the other components. For example, one blogger explains that their dropshipping business uses a web store, supply chain, and good marketing for success.

This same blogger insists that with those three components, you can even set up a dropshipping business in as little as a single day.

However, it is ill-advised to take such advice as you must spend time choosing between suppliers, exploring your options in a well-designed web store or site, and planning your marketing and promotions to ensure you are as competitive and profitable as possible.

So, how do you create a successful dropshipping enterprise? You blend those two lists. Doing so will guarantee you the least stressful setup, planning, and launching. In the sections that follow, we are going to look at:

- Identifying your products
- Choosing suppliers and building a dependable supply chain
- Creating your website and web store
- Marketing

These points will provide you with the best way to begin your career as a successful drop shipper. If you are ready, let's get started!

PART TWO

The Necessary Steps

If you explore what the experts have to say about dropshipping, most agree that selecting your niche and the products to sell can be one of the most healthy choices. You already know it is a competitive way of doing business, and that margins can be minimal. So, what this tells you is that the wiser your choice in products, the better your outcome.

Naturally, you can choose the perfect products and create a flawless store, but unless you can market effectively, you won't make many sales. We are going to consider all of these things like your most necessary steps.

Identifying Your Products

If we take a bit of advice from the professionals, we see that most will tell you to avoid choosing a niche or product based entirely on your interests or passions. As one group says: "This is an acceptable strategy if being interested in the product is your primary objective, not necessarily business success. But if your #1 goal is to build a profitable dropshipping site, you'll want to consider setting your passions aside when doing market research..." (Shopify) This may change if you find that the products that you love or are passionate about meeting the criteria for choosing your niche, but for the most part, your decisions have to based on the following issues. (Note: There is no such thing as the perfect niche or product, but doing the research takes you towards the most reliable choices.) To sell successfully, you will need to control pricing as much as possible. You can do this by making your goods, which then takes you out of dropshipping and is not something we'll cover in this guide.

Alternately, you can arrange for exclusive prices or make arrangements as a limited distributor. This shrinks the market and gives you a chance at more significant margins. If you cannot make such arrangements, sell at the lowest price possible, but not so small that you put yourself out of business. Instead, differentiate yourself by increasing the value of your product through tactics not related to the price.

For example, don't JUST dropship, but also provide information (free eBooks, web pages with authoritative or appealing content, and so on). Make it a joy to shop through your store, show you are providing buyers with answers to their needs or problems, and build complimentary inventory. As an example, you think it would be good to sell a high-quality skincare product, and you know there is a market for this, but to guarantee your ongoing success you need to determine how to trade multiple kinds of skincare products. Rather than marketing one product, selling a range of goods applied in various steps throughout the day or as part of a multi-step regimen (i.e., cleansing, toning, moisturizing, etc.) will ensure a complementary range of goods. Then, you can add value by offering free guides on optimal skin care, and so on. Products with Increased Value Are Ideal Some of the primary methods of increasing value without adding to the cost of goods or business include:

- Buyer guides
- Better and more explanatory product descriptions in entirely written English
- How to or setup guides
- Video guides
- Comparison tables and guides for the products sold

Use these ideas to help you find your niche, but also keep the intended audience in mind. For example, most drop shipping experts say that repeat buyers, hobbyists, and businesses are the best demographics from which to choose your niche. As an example, you might sell natural supplements to fitness centers. This means your clients are the fitness centers, but you also have the individuals using the products as part of the market. Repeat buyers on all fronts! However, if your product is consumable or disposable, you can also ensure that you can build a base of repeat buyers too. This is particularly true when many dropshipping professionals use sites like Amazon.com and its "Subscribe & Save" feature that essentially promises ongoing sales! Also, consider products that have many components or additional items. As an example, cell phones need cases, chargers, screen protectors, and more. Most buyers will stay within the same web store when they purchase goods, so always keep those complementary and accessory goods in mind when identifying your niche. You can also steer yourself towards the right products by visualizing how you are going to market them. Is it something you can easily imagine doing? Are there different ways you can see yourself writing or promoting the products? If so, you are probably on the right track. You can also choose a product or niche that is tough to find in your area. It could be almost anything, but if it is hard to get, it will usually have a market.

Choosing Suppliers and Building a Dependable Supply Chain

The supply chain is a term you can use to describe how the goods you sell go from manufacturing to your buyers. Your part in this "chain" is as a service provider as well as a retailer. You are not a manufacturer who creates goods and sells them to wholesalers or retailers. You are not a wholesaler who is going to purchase bulk quantities to sell to retailers. Instead, you are a retailer. You sell to the public at a markup. The big issue to take away from this explanation is that not everyone who says they are a wholesaler is one...they could be a retailer selling to you under false terms. In other words, choosing your suppliers and creating a functional supply chain that runs from the manufacturer to your buyers means doing some research. A firm that calls itself a wholesaler or even a dropshipper may be charging too much.

As one website warns, "it's critical to know how to differentiate between legitimate wholesale suppliers and retail stores posing as wholesale suppliers. A true wholesaler buys directly from the manufacturer and will usually be able to offer you significantly better pricing." Since it is your margins that will make or break your business, take the time to recognize the fakers. How? Most will ask you to pay a series of regular "fees" such as a monthly business fee or some ongoing financial obligation. This is completely illegitimate. Another warning sign is any firm that sells directly to the public. This makes them a retailer and not a wholesaler or drop shipper.

You can expect to pay a dependable dropshipping firm per order fees, and you may be required to meet their minimum order sizes. In other words, to create credit with them, you may need to pre-pay for a few hundred dollars worth of product. This is not uncommon, but it may also not be required. How do you find the valid drop shippers or wholesalers? There are several paths that can lead you to accurate dropshipping and wholesale suppliers:

Use Directories - These are databases of suppliers that are usually arranged by niche or product. Some of the biggest names include Doba, Worldwide Brands, SaleHoo, Wholesale Central, GoGo Dropship Directory, Note that some of them ask for monthly access fees, and this is not the same as the fees we mentioned above. In this case, you are paying for access to the database, and that is entirely valid.

Directly contact manufacturers - You can locate a legitimate wholesaler quickly if you get in touch with a company to find out who wholesales their goods.

Use the Internet - We now "Google" everything, and you can also use this search engine to find wholesalers. The best way is to put your search terms in brackets, i.e., "all-natural supplements for weight lifters wholesalers" and then be prepared to dig deep into the search results.

Go to a trade show - Once you know your niche or market, you can easily find trade shows and meet the wholesalers and manufacturers in person. Discuss your needs and ask all of the questions you have, and use this as an ideal opportunity for getting into contact with most of your industry suppliers.

Order from your competitors - If you are struggling to find wholesalers or valid dropshippers, place an order through one or more of your competitors. The shipping label will have the original shipping address, and you can use that to "Google" the name of the company. Once you have suppliers and can begin to know what you will earn from sales, it is time to start to create your actual business. Most of the sellers or suppliers will not sell to you unless you are an authentic and legal business entity. These firms are going to be able quickly to process your orders, package and ship them, include an invoice and label that features your name and logo, and even handle returns. You will receive the order through the web store, place that order with the supplier and pay them for it, and that is it! First, though, you must create the business and build the online store. Creating Your Store or Sales Channel When you are sure that your niche is profitable and that you will be able to market and sell the goods, you can take the next steps forward. This includes choosing the business structure you will use and registering your business name. You must then create a web presence. You can do this in two ways - building a store or site OR using an available web channel. The most common channels are eBay and Amazon.

Both provide you with live audiences, nearly instant startup processes, and less need for marketing. Both also have their downsides that include fees, the obligation to monitor and relist, no customization, no customer relationships, and to hand over your sales data to a company like Amazon. That means you can build your online store. This gives more control, allows you to customize the look, avoid fees, and create a relationship with customers. In other words, it is more of authentic business. Because of that, naturally, it is more involved were setup and commitment of time are concerned. Hobbyists tend to use eBay and Amazon, while those who are serious about building their business over the long term will create a store or site. Many also end up using all of the sales channels! To make your website, you need to tackle the following:

- Setting up a real business
- Getting a domain name
- Arranging web hosting and setting up the site - this is a big undertaking that includes listing products, using detailed descriptions, arranging for the payment options, dealing with taxes and shipping integration, and so on.
- Managing the site

It can be tough to get a business name and web URL or domain name that are a perfect match. However, you want always to choose a domain name that sounds trustworthy and not "fly by night." As a perfect example, consider something like naturalskincare.com (which is a randomly created domain name) versus something like skincreem4u.biz (also randomly created). The first one is more appealing and trustworthy and a good model to use when looking for the domain. In general, choose a domain name that is relevant, simple and short, easy to remember and type, professional and available. How do you get a domain? There are web-hosting services in great abundance.

Many provide you with package deals that allow you to register the domain name and provide you with the platform upon which your site is built and kept up and running. While GoDaddy is one of the biggest names in the world of domain names and hosting, there are many others. HostGator, DreamHost, Hostwinds, Liquid Web, 1&1 Web Hosting, Bluehost, HostMonster, and SiteGround are all comparable options, and there are even more to try. Explore user reviews and be sure that they work with WordPress. This is a framework for blogs, web stores, and websites and is removes all of the codings that was once essential for a website to operate. If a web hosting service is designed properly, it will allow you to install WordPress with a single click and provide you with fast speeds and a high percentage of uptime (meaning multiple servers that ensure your site is never down or unavailable).

After choosing a domain, getting your web hosting and installing WordPress, you will have to choose a theme. Though you can skip it, your site is going to be far too plain to generate attention and sales. That makes it the time to choose a theme. There are scores of theme providers, some offering free options and some asking for very reasonable rates.

The themes you will want to use are those with eCommerce plugins that allow you to create an online store easily. After you begin to build the site, it is time to consider the details of marketing. This is a bit more involved in the world of online sales, but it can be one of the most fun and exciting elements of dropshipping as a career. Before we move to that, though, one word of wisdom is to consider the use of a multichannel inventory and order management software package or service.

Dropshipping is now becoming a tactic that online retailers use to build their portfolio of sales channels. This is a bit more complex than a single dropshipping business. If you are interested in easily managing more than a single sales channel, such as a web store as a dropshipper and a sales page at Amazon or eBay, you may want to explore options for multichannel inventory and order management.

Additionally, as a business professional with a web presence of any kind (including your eBay or Amazon stores), you can use standard online marketing methods to draw traffic to your pages. The most straightforward methods include:

- Social media
- Blogging
- Email marketing
- Videos
- Printed material like posters and flyers
- PPC ads and banner ads
- Partnerships with complementary dropshipping professionals
- Hosting or participating in events and shows
- Participating in affiliate programs
- Word of mouth

- Value added material like free eBooks, guides, and that allow you to gather emails or phone numbers for further marketing
- SEO

We need to consider that last point in a bit of detail. That is because SEO is the one way to ensure you enjoy online success in your dropshipping endeavors. It is the one sure way to keep traffic headed to your site and is what you will find yourself doing roughly 75% of the time during the first few months you are in business. It is too complicated to teach you to do here, but you will need to spend time learning which keywords are the most potent for your niche, and then use them in everything from page titles and product descriptions to social media posts and your actual web pages.

A simple guide for beginners is available for free at Moz.com, and it is considered to be one of the best beginner's guides to the use of SEO. Entitled The Beginners Guide to SEO, it is a good place to learn about this marketing technique and begin applying to all of your dropshipping pages, sites, and materials.

ADVANTAGES AND DISADVANTAGES OF DROPSHIPPING

Below, I'll outline the benefits and disadvantages of drop shipping versus a traditional retail business. So you can get a sense of how it is like to run a dropshipping business in real-life.

Advantages

Zero Capital Required to Get Started – I was a student without a dime to my name when I launched my dropshipping business (I shared previously how we started eBay dropshipping with zero cash). You don't need to buy any product inventory upfront, and you only pay the supplier a portion of what you get from the customer.

Work from Anywhere – Having suppliers drop ship for you, basically means you have partners taking care of all physical aspects of running your business, while you're in charge of the digital aspects – listing products, marketing, optimizing, supporting customers, etc.

After a year or so of running our small dropshipping business, Max, Dima (our first employee) and I realized we could work from anywhere in the world as long as we had a Wifi connection. And so, we packed our laptops and flew to work from Dubrovnik, Croatia (where many Games of Thrones scenes where filmed!).

Scalability – Whether you're dropshipping a $1 mobile phone case or a $2,000 piece of furniture, the amount of work for you is the same, you need to transfer the order information to your supplier. This means that a dropshipping business is highly scalable and is virtually only limited by the processing capacity of your suppliers. Even then, if your suppliers have limited stock or can't handle the volume of your orders, you can source another dropship supplier.

After being hit by "Out of stock" problems on several occasions, Max and I started to insure ourselves by striving to have at least one alternative drop ship supplier for every line of product we offered.

We were also much more careful when choosing dropshipping suppliers, in some cases traveling abroad to meet them face to face.

Endless Selection of Products – Not need to purchase or store your inventory, means that you can offer a wide variety of products and let the sales data drive your business expansion.

Disadvantages

High Risk – All physical aspects of the business are out of your hands. While you must commit to a high packaging quality, quick handling and shipping times and stock availability, all of these aspects are out of your control, and you need to rely on your dropship suppliers, who are often from the other side of the world and have a different business culture than yours.

There are a lot of moving parts which are out of your hands. It can be very frustrating having to communicate with angry customers because your supplier messed up his role.

Low-Profit Margins – The entry barrier to the dropshipping world is relatively small, which means that it's a very crowded space. This is especially true during the last few years. Take a look at this google trends graph, showing interest in dropshipping over time:

Dropshipping is booming in recent years. Sellers must find a unique competitive advantage to stand above the competition and generate substantial revenues.

I'll repeat it – dropshipping, like any other business, is damn hard. Only the stubborn, focused, and determined will succeed.

Slower Shipping Times – According to studies, shipping time is a top factor in online shoppers buying decision. It won't be long before Amazon flies its drones to your doorstep with the package you've just ordered a few hours or even minutes ago. Dropshipping your orders from suppliers instead of managing your logistics usually means slower shipping times.

In Conclusion

This introduction to dropshipping should help you begin to identify your ideal niche and product, determine whether you want to be a full-time professional with a web store and site or someone who piggybacks on the ease of Amazon or eBay to get started. It will help you take the right steps where marketing is concerned, but you will find that there is much more to learn. Dropshipping is a simplified and affordable way to get started in a business of your own, but take this guide as a basic introduction. Commit time to research and learn all about your available markets and products, explore the most authentic wholesalers and drop shippers, and make solid plans to enjoy the best outcomes. The best of luck to you in this exciting endeavor.

AMAZON FBA

SECTION THREE

INTRODUCTION TO AMAZON FBA

Amazon's FBA program is an excellent opportunity for the vast audience of entrepreneurs. Especially those that are starting out as a one man shop. What's remarkable with Amazon FBA is its scalability. As a one man shop, you can compete with the bigger and more established seller. Small businesses are limited in storage space and the time management to sell, list, make and ship orders. You can fulfill small orders (ex. 20 per day) as well as the larger orders (ex. 100,000 per day). Which translate that you can start out as a mom and pop shop and flourish as a larger corporate using Amazaon's Fulfillment. You can now handle the increased volume in an efficient way while managing your inventory and spending your to source your product.

This will reduce the competitive advantage of the bigger seller and enable you to make a real income and grow as big as you desire. Think about it. You just need access to your product(s) of choice. Amazon FBA provides a stream of income that you can take to a whole new level. At each fulfillment center, (Amazon has over 65) you are hiring at LOW rates per order a staff that takes care of the order processing, shipping and customer.

What is Amazon FBA?

As a business owner or individual who is looking to sell products via Amazon, having the opportunity to take advantage of Fulfillment By Amazon can be quite beneficial. With the ability to minimize the amount of time that you would spend selling and shipping your products, Fulfillment By Amazon does most of the work for you. If you're currently interested in these services, below is information and how it can be useful for your selling needs.

The Fulfillment Process

The entire process is relatively simple. You will be provided the opportunity to store your products in one of Amazon's fulfillment centers. Once a customer purchases something that you have for sale, they will pick, pack, and ship it for you. Also, customer service will be allotted to each product that you are looking to sell. That means that if your buyer has any questions, customer service will handle the questions.

Fees

Another significant benefit associated with using Amazon FBA is that you will be able to take advantage of their services for a minimal fee. As a more cost-effective solution than opening your warehouse and packing/shipping your goods, you can eliminate this time-consuming task without having to pay outrageous fees. You will be able to pay as you go when you start working with Amazon. Each company will be charged by the space that you use in the warehouse and the number of orders that Amazon fulfills.

What to Sell Using Amazon FBA

One of the most significant advantages associated with using Amazon's Fulfillment to sell your goods is that dozens of different categories let you know what to sell. The majority of sellers list their products in the "Open Categories" section because listing products under these categories do not require approval. Some of the Open Categories available to companies include:

- Amazon Kindle
- Books
- Baby Products
- Cameras and Photos
- Cell Phones
- Home and Garden
- Accessories for Electronics

The other categories available for people wondering what to sell using Amazon FBA are known as "Professional Seller Categories." To list your products here, you will require approval. Some of these categories include:

- Automotive & Powersports
- Beauty
- Collectible Coins
- Clothing & Accessories
- Fine Art
- Gift Cards
- Grocery & Gourmet Food

These are just a few helpful tips and hints to assist you as you move forward with your fulfillment business.

TIPS FOR PICKING A WINNING PRODUCT

Finding the right products to sell on Amazon is vitally important. Find a winning product, and it will almost sell itself. However, try to launch something that is too competitive or something that no one wants, and you'll find yourself at the bottom of the pile of hundreds of other Amazon sellers. These abbreviated steps will help you get on the right track:

1. Existing successful products? You want to make sure people are currently buying the product you are interested in selling. If you can go into a "hot" market, you are much more likely to pick up some market sales (i.e., make sales).
2. Start small yet profitable: The easiest way to keep your costs down and to test ideas quickly is to order a product in small batches. Order as few units as the manufacturer will agree to so you can test it out. Be

more concerned with profit margins after all fees than the actual size of the product.

3. Can I make it better? I prefer to find a unique feature or improvement I can make to existing products so my listing will stand out. Get ideas from negative reviews and creative thinking.

4. Can I compete? Always look to see how many reviews the products on page 1 have. If they all have hundreds of reviews, it might be tough to compete. However, if some have only a handful of reviews, that means you can rank quickly.

5. Keep it simple: The more complicated your product, the more it will cost to get started. It also gives more chances for something to go wrong. Start by looking for simple products that don't require complicated tooling or engineering.

Steps to Finding, Manufacturing and Selling Products with Amazon FBA

1. Find products that sell well currently on Amazon using Jungle Scout and the steps listed above. If existing products don't sell well, I move on to another idea.
2. Look for ways to improve/change product to make it unique based on negative feedback in their reviews.
3. Order samples and modify as needed to get your product right, and then place your order.
4. Find a logistics company to help import your goods and deliver them to Amazon's fulfillment center
5. Take high-quality pictures and a keyword-rich title and description on Amazon based on your keyword research.
6. Discount products to break-even or even less to start getting sales on your product. If using third party

promotional tools to promote your discounts, make sure they comply with Amazon's terms of service

7. Automate follow-up and get ongoing reviews using SalesBacker.

8. After your product starts selling, create a website, and use long-tail keywords to drive even more traffic to your products. I use Long Tail Pro to help with this.

9. If you're successful, look to add similar products to your portfolio and increase sales by repeating the process.

Tools I Use For FBA

- Jungle Scout - This is how I check the sales numbers of competing products on Amazon and determine if it is worth creating a similar product of my own.

- Long Tail Pro - Discover keywords to target in my title and get ideas about the kinds of products people are looking for.

- AMZTracker - II use this to track where my products are ranking for the keywords I'm targeting on Amazon, I've also used it to manage promos and discounts on a larger scale.
- SalesBacker - This automates my follow-up with buyers, reminding them to come back andleave a review, so my product continues to rank better in Amazon.
- Thrive Leads - Once my website is setup. Thrive Leads has helped me capture email addresses of potential buyers and communicate with them via email. I also use Thrive to ask my visitors questions and match them up with the best item from my line of products.
- Scott Voelker Coaching - Scott has built a thriving Amazon FBA business, and I've learned quite a bit from him. If you'd like a coach to help you succeed, I highly recommend Scott.

Remember Your Margins

It's easy to get excited about an idea and then overlook the importance of having enough profit margin. Your manufacturing, shipping, import, and FBA costs all add up - so make sure you can still earn a healthy profit before placing your order. Having razor-thin profit margins is a recipe for failure - so no matter how much you love a particular idea, always double and triple check your margins. Here is a link to the FBA calculator where you can get an idea of what your FBA fees will be by searching an item that is similar size/weight to yours. I like to shoot for 30 to 40% profit margins.

Benefits of Selling FBA

- Creating revenue can happen much faster than other online businesses, such as starting a new niche website

- It's hands-off - meaning you don't have to store and ship your products or deal with returns
- Your products are Prime eligible, which means people will pay more for the assurance of fast, free shipping from Amazon
- You don't have to worry about generating traffic - Amazon draws plenty of it, and you can tap into their enormous customer base.

Why is FBA a Big Deal?

Perhaps the most obvious beneficiaries of FBA are small business owners, who likely don't have efficient fulfillment systems in place and don't want to risk the potential adverse effects that poor customer experience could instigate. For this reason, Amazon is a very favorable business partner. Professional Amazon sellers see the bigger picture, namely: FBA inventory's eligibility for Amazon Prime Its influential role on Buy Box ownership The added safeguard for other significant Buy Box factors like Fulfillment Latency and Seller Rating The benefit that FBA represents a seller's brand in a more positive light.

There is a robust correlation between FBA utilization and higher sales performance While there are a right amount of professional Amazon sellers who FBA 100% of their inventory, this isn't to say that every third-party seller should do this. One of the goals of this white paper is to paint FBA as a very immediate, strategic tool sellers should deploy only for the listings it makes sense for. A common misconception is that sellers should either be 100% FBM or 100% FBA, yet most professional Amazon sellers are an FBA/FBM hybrid. Not every product a seller offers will be the right candidate for FBA for a variety of reasons, mainly size, sales performance, and margin. Knowing which listings it makes sense for is called FBA inventory selection, and this will be covered later in the guide.

Why Is the Buy Box So Important? The Buy Box is the single most essential piece of "property" on the Amazon marketplace. With 82% of Amazon website sales going through the Buy Box and an even more significant figure in Amazon mobile sales, the Buy Box is seen as the critical opportunity for online marketplace sellers today to increase their selling potential. Sellers must learn about how the Buy Box works and how Amazon determines who "wins" this coveted spot. So what motivates Amazon when it comes to choosing who wins the Buy Box? Put, Amazon will always favor offers that are most customer-friendly and consequently, the most likely to be purchased. Amazon prides itself on the company's extremely high levels of customer service. Amazon's whole essence focuses around offering the best possible experience to their customers. It is for this reason that the Buy Box was created to compare multiple offerings of the same product to determine which will provide the customer with the highest levels of satisfaction. To Amazon, this means the offers with the best price, fulfillment method, seller rating, etc. The Amazon Buy Box winner is determined by an algorithm that aims to give the customer the best possible value. It does this by first determining which product offering meets all the necessary minimum requirements. It then breaks down each available offering into many different variables and uses them to find the seller who offers the best balance between high seller performance and low-cost price.

How to Avoid Long Term Storage Fees A semi-annual Long-Term Storage Fee will be applied to any units that have been stored in an Amazon fulfillment center for six months or longer. Units that have been in an Amazon fulfillment center for six to 12 months as of the Inventory Cleanup date will be charged $11.25 per cubic foot. Units that have been in an Amazon fulfillment center for 12 months as of the Inventory Cleanup date will be billed $22.50 per cubic foot. The Long-Term Storage Fee is in addition to the regular

Inventory Storage Fee and will not be charged if a removal order has been created to remove or dispose of the units before the Fee being charged. Each seller may maintain a single unit of each ASIN in its inventory, which will be exempt from the semi-annual Long-Term Storage Fee. Why Does Amazon Charge FBA Long Term Storage Fees?

According to Amazon, a stock that is overstocked or stored indefinitely in their fulfillment centers limits their ability to provide space for fast-selling products customers want. The Long-Term Storage Fee program helps ensure that they can continue to provide high levels of service to all sellers and provide customers with products that they want. Amazon doesn't anticipate sellers will store merchandise in Amazon fulfillment centers for long periods, but in the event, this does happen—sellers can suffer significantly at the expense of these high additional costs. There is a cost for long-term storage space, and that cost is not built into their monthly storage cost structure.

1. Discover Which Products Are at Risk for FBA Storage Fees The first step for retailers to avoid extra fees is assessing their FBA inventory to determine which products are at risk for accruing long term fees. Amazon sellers can access the Inventory Health report before an Inventory Cleanup date to estimate the number of units that are susceptible to long term fees within the fulfillment centers for six months to 12 months or 12 months or longer.

According to Amazon, these units would be subject to the Long-Term Storage Fee (minus any units that sell before then). When calculating Fees in the Profitability Analysis, sellers should be aware that: FBA fees are not calculated off the price of an item. If sellers are over 30% in feed, they should be increasingly aware of their margins Fee is unit-based (this will differ across catalog), so ASIN-level approach is required You can access the Inventory Health report in Seller Central (sign-in required) by going to Reports > Fulfillment > Inventory > Inventory Health and requesting a download.

2. Increase Sales Velocity Through Pricing Strategy
Some sellers might be wondering if it's a good idea to invest the time to reprice and try to sell their products before August 15th? Repricing is powerful. It has to be the right competitive landscape for it – you might be limited by MAP or by your margins. Assuming you have a handle on all those factors, repricing is a way to increase that velocity.

3. Request a Removal Order to Avoid FBA Storage Fees
The Recommended Removal report provides an

interface in a seller's account to more easily identify and remove units that are at risk of being assessed the Long-Term Storage Fee. This report will auto-calculate on an ASIN-by-ASIN basis the number of units you need to remove (assuming no further sales of your inventory) to avoid the Long-Term Storage Fee and will prepopulate a removal request for those units if you choose to remove them. The report only shows units that are at risk of being assessed fees within six weeks of each cleanup date.

You can access the Recommended Removal report in Seller Central (sign-in required) by going to Reports > Fulfillment > Inventory > Recommended Removal and requesting a download. Once that removal order is in your account, Amazon will exclude that inventory from your long term storage fee. They will try to send those orders back to you in bulk. So that inventory can take a week to two weeks to get back to you, depending on how much you are requesting.

THE PROS & CONS OF FBA

The decision of whether or not to fulfill through Amazon should not be made on a whim. Sellers must evaluate many different factors in their decision-making process, since what may be right for one seller may not be the correct way to go for another. Sellers may also decide that some of their products may be suitable for FBA, but others are more appropriate to fulfill themselves. The selling points to FBA are many.

The Pros Convenience FBA relieves the seller of a potentially large headache. Amazon's fulfillment centers store the seller's products and do all the legwork for them. When an order is received, Amazon's employees pick, pack and ship the products, plus they'll deal with all the customer service queries and returns. Eligibility With FBA, a seller's products are eligible for Super Saver Shipping, Amazon Prime and Buy Box Eligible status, which all lead to a higher conversion rate. The Amazon Reputation Many believe that customers are more likely to buy from a seller who has the Amazon name attached to them. This is due to the strong level of trust that the company inspires in them. If something goes wrong, people know that Amazon will take care of it. They also know Amazon has mastered the distribution process and will send the item quickly. Sales Performance There's also the argument that FBA sellers can sell more because they have the Amazon name attached to them. For example, let's say a seller has ten boxes of coffee and is selling them from home at $42 + $8 for shipping. They would have to go to the post office and pay to ship each sale individually, including the materials to put the coffee in.

On the other hand, if they were selling FBA, they could ship all the boxes to Amazon in one go and then list them at $50 each with free shipping. So the cost to the customer would be the same, but as an FBA seller, they would be making more profit. The Cons Fees Using FBA can be extremely costly, particularly for large products. Often a seller may have the workforce and willpower to be taking care of certain elements themselves, so switching to FBA could hike their costs up. However, as noted earlier, using FBA doesn't necessarily mean that a seller will be expensing more to be able to sell a product on the Amazon Marketplace. FBA fees are in a place of a seller's normal operational and fulfillment costs. Commingling When using FBA, Amazon's fulfillment centers will ask that the seller identifies their products using unique product identifiers. Commingling inventory is essentially the process of pooling Seller A's units with Seller B's units of the same UPC at an Amazon fulfillment center. If a seller chooses not to label their inventory, commingling is a potential con for FBA because fake products from other sellers can enter the mix. This opens the door to the possibility that a customer purchases a product from you and receives the fake version from another seller—a high risk for products like sunglasses. Other risks include the product from another seller being damaged or faulty. However, there are some upsides to embracing commingling. The "It Depends" While there are both clear advantages and disadvantages to FBA that may sway a seller in either direction, the discussion is a lot less straightforward, and the following must be taken into account by each seller considering FBA. It Depends What You Sell Although some of the fees associated with FBA change according to product size and weight, the pick & pack handling fees are fixed. Therefore, if items tend to be relatively small, not too heavy, and sell at higher prices, it makes the FBA fees more manageable.

For example, a $10 item that is large and heavy will represent a large percentage of your margin, whereas the fees for a small and light item that sells at $30, will represent a much smaller percentage. For this reason, high ASP (average sale price) is a big consideration for FBA inventory selection. Popular items that sell quickly are also great for FBA. It does not make sense to send something to Amazon that isn't likely to sell and may languish in storage, racking up storage fees. While some sellers dispute this by claiming that low sales rank items are ideal to sell via FBA, since their chances of selling usually go up quite a bit due to their Amazon Prime "teaser," it's a high-risk move that makes a seller vulnerable to very costly storage fees. As a side note, sellers should be aware of the fact that storage fees increase during busy periods like Q4. It Depends How Much You Sell For high-volume sellers, physical storage space could be an issue which FBA would solve. The higher the turnover rate for your inventory, the more storage space Amazon will grant you.

For growing sellers, FBA could also be useful since their workload would decrease significantly, freeing up their time to focus on growing their business. It Depends How Much Manpower You Have FBA could prove extremely useful to a seller who lacks the workforce to cope with an overabundance of orders. Fulfilling an item oneself involves going to the post office or engaging with a shipping carrier, and with people expecting quick shipping, a seller would need to be ready to fulfill their order within a day or two.

Taking on extra employees would involve managing a fleet of employees, which a seller might not want. It is also sometimes difficult to judge when there will be an influx of orders, and therefore hard to prepare the necessary workforce in advance.

So Is FBA Worth It?

The answer is that a seller needs to know their business. They need to have an in-depth knowledge of their inventory and invoices and be able to assess which listings it makes sense for strategically.

www.ingramcontent.com/pod-product-compliance
Lightning Source LLC
Chambersburg PA
CBHW030642220526
45463CB00004B/1609